Original title:
Dreaming in Art

Copyright © 2024 Swan Charm Publishing
All rights reserved.

Editor: Jessica Elisabeth Luik
Author: Paulina Pähkel
ISBN HARDBACK: 978-9916-86-170-7
ISBN PAPERBACK: 978-9916-86-171-4

Celestial Brushstrokes

Stars cascade in twilight's embrace,
Galactic hues in cosmic space.
Auroras dance, the heavens glow,
In night's majestic, silent show.

Nebulae swirl in colors bright,
Sketching dreams in the canvas of night.
Planets whisper, moons gleam,
In cosmic art, a timeless theme.

Fleeting Figments

Memories drift like autumn leaves,
In the mind, where time weaves.
Moments grasped, then soon they fly,
Like whispers lost in the sighing sky.

Echoes of laughter, shades of tears,
A tapestry woven through the years.
Glimpses vanish, shadows play,
In the dance of night and day.

Surreal Silhouettes

Shadows twist in moonlit glade,
Silent dreams in starlight wade.
Figures form in twilight's beam,
A surreal, enchanting dream.

Whispered tales in midnight air,
Fades the line between the fair.
Luminous silhouettes entwine,
In a realm beyond design.

Escapades in Acrylic

Brush strokes weave a vivid tale,
Colors burst, where dreams sail.
Imaginations take their flight,
On canvas realms of pure delight.

Hues collide in vibrant spree,
Crafting worlds for eyes to see.
Artistry both wild and free,
In acrylic's grand decree.

Outre Oeuvres

In realms where shadows play and light does twirl,
Beyond our reach, creations yet unfurled,
An artist's hand, with strokes both bold and pure,
Crafts visions from a world that won't demur.

Canvas stretches wide, an untold lore,
Whispers from beyond its woven core,
Colors bloom like galaxies in flight,
Stories come alive in spectral light.

Echoes of a time that never was,
Blend with dreams and cosmic laws,
Infinite in scope, both grand and small,
A masterpiece that transcends us all.

Through the silence, faintly, voices sing,
Of untamed dreams and everything,
An oeuvre from the heart, unbound, unique,
In foreign tongues, these wonders speak.

Beyond the veil of known and unknown,
A world where pure imagination's sown,
Outre oeuvres, where reality refrains,
In night's quiet, their legacy remains.

Augmented Realities in Paint

Brush meets canvas in a digital haze,
A fusion of old and new for the gaze,
Pixels blend, a dance between the lines,
Reality shifts, redefined by signs.

Augmented visions draped in vivid hues,
Alternate worlds emerge with subtle cues,
Through a screen, the cosmos intertwines,
Art transcends, beyond the physical confines.

Layered textures tell a silent story,
Virtuoso crafts a scene of glory,
Boundaries blur in the electric heat,
In painted realms where old and new do meet.

Shadows fade and colors start to bend,
Infinite paths within the trends,
In augmented views, truths intertwine,
A modern canvas, endlessly divine.

From thought to screen, an artist's dream bestowed,
A universe within and outflows,
Augmented realities in paint unfurl,
A digital masterpiece, beyond this world.

Artistic Asleep

Brushstrokes blend in twilight's keep,
Colors swirl in silent sweep.
Dreamscapes form in shadows deep,
Artists muse while slumbered sleep.

Canvas whispers, secrets shared,
Imagination, unprepared.
Abstract visions, none compared,
To dreams where thought is truly spared.

Palette's hues in nighttime's veil,
Sketch life's tales in moon's detail.
Creativity sets sail,
In dreams where sleep does softly trail.

Brush and Beyond

Canvas primed with morning's dew,
Every stroke a world anew.
Lines and shapes in varied hue,
Beyond the brush, a soul's debut.

Textures rise from depths unknown,
Drawing life from seeds they've sown.
In each mark, a feeling's shown,
In worlds of art, the heart is known.

Colors dance, a vibrant tale,
On horizons, dreams prevail.
Creativity lifts its sail,
Brush and beyond, no set travail.

Past Midnight Panels

Midnight hour, silence reigns,
Art unfurls in shadowed lanes.
Panel lights with ink sustains,
Memories drawn in secret chains.

Figures glide on darkened sheet,
Stories told in quiet retreat.
Lines converge where thoughts compete,
Past midnight, the tales repeat.

Canvas dark, yet visions gleam,
Art becomes a silent dream.
On these panels, worlds redeem,
Past midnight, nothing's as it seems.

Surrealist Sleep

Eyes closed, a world redefined,
Surreal dreams in sleep confined.
Abstract realms with time entwined,
Where reason fades, and thoughts unwind.

Shapes and forms in chaos thrive,
Sleep's embrace where visions dive.
Reality's laws cease to survive,
In dreams where fantasies arrive.

Colors shift in endless play,
Night and day in disarray.
Surrealist sleep leads the way,
Through dreams where wonders softly sway.

Sleep-Tinted Reality

Moonlight whispers through the trees,
As shadows paint our reverie,
Stars compose a silent plea,
In a sleep-tinted reality.

Dreams unfold like ancient lore,
Echoing in heart and core,
Softly knocking on night's door,
Eager for just one dream more.

Clouds drift by in twilight's hue,
Woven in a sky of blue,
Memories that we pursue,
Fade in morning's first light, too.

Nighttime's veil begins to lift,
Reality begins to shift,
In the dawn, our spirits drift,
With each gentle morning gift.

Dream Drafts

In the quiet of the night,
Whispers of dreams take their flight,
Gathering in sleepy light,
Crafting worlds off in the night.

Pages of an unseen book,
In the dreamscape, come and look,
Thoughts and hopes in every nook,
Boundless fields all undertook.

Characters brought forth in sleep,
In our minds they deeply seep,
Promising us secrets deep,
For our hearts to find and keep.

In each draft, a realm unknown,
Born in twilight's softened tone,
In the light, we stand alone,
Yet in dreams, it's all re-shown.

Mystic Mosaics

Fragments of a mystic night,
Gather in the pale moonlight,
Forming shapes that don't seem right,
Yet they hold a secret sight.

Pieces of a cosmic dance,
In a world where dreams enhance,
Every glance a fleeting chance,
In this mystic trance, we prance.

Colors blend and softly clash,
Every thought a fleeting flash,
On this canvas, smiles dash,
Stories told in dreamlike splash.

Every night, anew they weave,
Mystic patterns we believe,
Until the dawn bids us leave,
Holding what the dreams conceive.

Chromatic Slumbers

Hues of twilight in the air,
Merge to form a slumber fair,
Colors vivid, bright, and rare,
Paint the dreams that gently flare.

Auroras of a midnight scheme,
Shade the contours of our dream,
In a deep chromatic stream,
Where the stars in whispers gleam.

Rainbows whisper through the night,
In each shade, a hidden light,
Promise of a world so bright,
Held in the soft grip of night.

Waking finds these hues replaced,
As the day our dreams erased,
Yet their memory we chased,
In colors that our sleep embraced.

Awakening the Imagination

In twilight's tender glow,
Ideas begin to flow.
Dreams take flight on wings,
Awakening hidden things.

Visions dance in the dark,
Igniting a creative spark.
Colors paint the mind,
In shadows, treasures we find.

Whispers of forgotten lore,
Enter through an open door.
Mysteries come alive,
In daydreams, we thrive.

Threads of thought entwine,
Stories seek to align.
Imagination's grand parade,
In our hearts, dreams are made.

Beyond the mundane sight,
Lies pure creative light.
A universe of fantasy,
Awakens eternally.

Transcendent Mosaics

Fragments of the soul,
Assembled into a whole.
Luminescent hues entwine,
Patterns of the divine.

Each piece holds a tale,
Of triumphs and travail.
Shadows and light embrace,
In a timeless, silent space.

Mosaic worlds unfold,
As secrets are retold.
Every shard a dream,
Flowing like a stream.

Symphonies of sight,
Born from eternal night.
Transcendence in each frame,
Ever-changing, yet the same.

Wholeness found in parts,
Mosaic of our hearts.
A dance of color and glass,
Where past and future pass.

Veils of Wonder

Beneath the night's embrace,
Magic claims its space.
Veils of wonder weave,
Believing hearts retrieve.

Stars whisper ancient songs,
To where each soul belongs.
Cosmic threads will bind,
Mysteries we find.

Auroras paint the skies,
With secrets in disguise.
Through the veils of night,
We grasp transcendent light.

Dreams awaken softly,
In realms that drift so lofty.
Behold, the world anew,
Where enchantment comes true.

Veils of wonder lift,
The soul begins to shift.
In endless night's embrace,
Magic leaves its trace.

Enchanted Easel

Upon the easel stand,
A world awaits my hand.
Brushstrokes bring to life,
Visions beyond strife.

Canvas whispers low,
Secrets few will know.
Colors swirl and dance,
In a timeless trance.

Palette rich and bright,
Crafts realms of pure delight.
From the heart's deep well,
Stories begin to tell.

Imagination ignites flame,
Creation plays its game.
Art's spell comes to weave,
Magic, we believe.

Enchanted easel shows,
The inner light that glows.
Every stroke a dream,
Flowing like a stream.

Dreamt Landscapes

Beneath the moon's soft silver glow,
Dreamt landscapes whisper secrets low.
Enchanted valleys, forests deep,
In slumber's hold, our spirits keep.

Mountains rise, a shadowed crest,
Upon their peaks our hopes do rest.
Rivers wind through meadows green,
A tranquil world, serene, unseen.

Starlit skies above the plains,
Whisper songs of gentle rains.
In glades where ancient trees have grown,
Dreams take flight, forever sown.

Ethereal Symphony

A symphony of stars, divine,
In cosmic rhythms so entwined.
Galaxies in silent dance,
Compose the heavens' vast expanse.

Celestial voices, pure and bright,
Sing of worlds beyond our sight.
Harmonic echoes, music's light,
Guide us through the endless night.

Planets orbit in their grace,
Time and space, a wondrous chase.
In the void where shadows flee,
An ethereal symphony.

Visions in Oils

Brushstrokes tell a tale untold,
Of dreams in colors bright and bold.
Canvas whispers secrets old,
In hues of crimson, blue, and gold.

Silent scenes of quiet grace,
Captured in a painter's space.
Each stroke a heartbeat, life embraced,
A timeless world in pigments traced.

With every layer, depths unfold,
A story laced in shadows cold.
Visions in oils, truth beheld,
In every hue, a soul is meld.

Fantasy on Canvas

On canvas pale, a world appears,
Of ancient tales and vanished years.
In strokes so bold, our dreams are laid,
A fantasy where time has stayed.

Dragons soar on skies of flame,
Heroes rise in quest for fame.
Myth and legend intertwine,
In every line, a tale divine.

Forests deep with shadows cast,
Magic woven from the past.
A realm where wonders never cease,
Fantasy on canvas—peace.

Sleepy Hues

In twilight's tender, dusky gloom,
Where stars emerge to softly bloom,
The world slips into sleepy hues,
A land where dreams commune.

Night wraps us in its silken thread,
A gentle lull in feathered bed,
While shadows dance in muted shoes,
In realms of rest and spread.

Whispers float on evening breeze,
Through parted curtains, past the trees,
Invoking silent, deep amuse,
In harmony with ease.

Eyes grow heavy as night deep,
Enfolding minds in tranquil keep,
In sleepy hues, the soul renews,
Embraced by night's vast sweep.

Painterly Phantasms

In the realm of endless dream,
Brushstrokes glint in moonlight's gleam,
Phantasms dance in painted streams,
A kaleidoscope of theme.

Colors swirl, a vibrant play,
In this canvas of the night,
A fantasy that fades with day,
But lingers, soft and bright.

Imagination takes its flight,
Through azure skies and emerald seas,
Each hue a whisper of delight,
In painterly reprise.

Shapes and forms that morph and bend,
In this dreamscape of design,
Where fantasies and realities blend,
On sleep's soft silken line.

The Art of Slumber

In dreams, an artist wields the brush,
Crafting scenes in tranquil hush,
A tapestry of whispered lore,
In slumber's gentle thrush.

With each stroke, a world is born,
Of shadowed night and breaking dawn,
In realms where weary spirits soar,
And earthly ties are shorn.

Stars are sprinkled like white pearls,
'Cross twilight's canvas, soft and wide,
In somnolent, enchanting swirls,
As consciousness subsides.

Through veils of sleep, adventures call,
In silent, flowing reverie,
The art of slumber, ever-all,
A boundless dreamer's sea.

Colors of Consciousness

Awakened mind where colors play,
In chromatic fields of thought,
Each hue a whisper, soft array,
In the tapestry time wrought.

Dawns of gold and nights of blue,
Blend in mental symphonies,
A vibrant dance in twilight's hue,
Of secret memories.

Emerald dreams and scarlet fears,
Merge in consciousness's embrace,
Through spectrum's sweep of years,
We find our place, our pace.

In waking hours, colors run,
Through veins of life's eternal thread,
Consciousness a vivid sun,
In mental landscapes spread.

Mirage of Strokes

In twilight's gentle hue,
They paint the dusk and dawn,
A language soft, yet true,
A canvas newly drawn.

Brushes dance and weave,
In whispers of the night,
What dreams might they achieve,
With every stroke of light?

Like shadows cast in gold,
They shimmer in the breeze,
Stories yet untold,
Unfold with subtle ease.

Through colors bright and bold,
A journey we embark,
A tale of love retold,
Eclipsing every arc.

Pastel Phantasms

Soft pastel visions blend,
In twilight's silent grace,
Where dreams and daylight mend,
Their gentle, warm embrace.

Whispers from a time,
In colors' tender sway,
Trace the paths of rhyme,
A gentle, muted play.

Ephemeral and rare,
These phantasms reside,
In the still midair,
Where thoughts and dreams collide.

Subtle hues confound,
In worlds beyond our grasp,
Lost and yet profound,
In memory's tender clasp.

Mind's Mirage

In the labyrinth of thought,
Echoes of dreams confined,
Where shadows are oft caught,
In corners of the mind.

Visions ebb and flow,
Through corridors unseen,
A celestial glow,
In ethereal sheen.

Lost in reverie's clasp,
Where time and space entwine,
In each mirage we grasp,
A fleeting, sacred sign.

Through the veils of mist,
In silent, whispering chimes,
Phantoms of the tryst,
Unfold in measured rhymes.

Tales in Tempera

On canvas rough and bare,
A saga starts to bloom,
Colors kissed with care,
Dispelling every gloom.

Scenes of yore emerge,
From strokes both proud and grand,
Where hues and moments surge,
In artisan's skilled hand.

Every tint and shade,
A fragment of the lore,
A story deftly made,
A past that we adore.

In tempera's embrace,
A chronicle takes flight,
Transcending time and space,
Immortal in its light.

Acrylic Aerials

In a sky brushed with hues of dream,
Pastel clouds in an azure stream.
Birds on wings of vivid grace,
Soar through fields of endless space.

Mountains rise in shades of mist,
Sunset's palette, dusk's gentle twist.
Oceans whisper secrets old,
Tales in aquamarine and gold.

Forests dance in emerald gleam,
Underneath a moonlit beam.
Stars above in patterns bright,
Canvas painted by the night.

Pictorial Phantasms

In frames of gold, the visions play,
A dance of light, a soft ballet.
Mirrors hold the spectral dream,
Whispers of a silent scream.

Brushes ink the fleeting thought,
Echoes of what time has sought.
Ghosts of past, in colors bold,
Stories that the eyes behold.

Painter's hand, with gentle care,
Crafts a world beyond compare.
Marvels caught in twilight's glow,
Secrets only paintings know.

Whimsical Worlds

Beyond the veil, where dreams entwine,
Lies a world of pure design.
Whimsies dance on rays of sun,
To realms where fancies run.

Mountains float on seas of light,
Flowers bloom in rainbow sight.
Butterflies in patterns spin,
Magic worlds, we wander in.

Laughing trees and singing streams,
Wild creatures birthed from dreams.
Here, in lands of joy so free,
Imagination forms the key.

Drowsy Design

In the hush of twilight's yawn,
Dreams emerge as day is gone.
Patterns weave in gentle sweep,
Lulling minds to realms of sleep.

Curtains drawn in shades of dusk,
Night's embrace, in whispers husk.
Stars align, in gentle glow,
Guiding where the dreamers go.

Pillows soft and covers tight,
Slip into the tranquil night.
Drowsy worlds of calm design,
Cradle souls in rest divine.

Imaginary Landscapes

In dreams, the flowers bloom anew,
Fields of azure, skies of gold,
Mountains rise in sapphire hue,
Stories of wonder yet untold.

Rivers whisper secrets deep,
Echoes of a time gone by,
Forests where the shadows sleep,
Underneath a twilight sky.

Stars dance in celestial cheer,
Winds weave tales of ancient lore,
Horizons never drawing near,
Endless realms to still explore.

Valleys hum a peaceful song,
Nature's symphony at play,
In this world where we belong,
Night gives birth to break of day.

Castles float on clouds of white,
Dreams take flight on feathered wings,
In this realm of pure delight,
Every heart in wonder sings.

Pastel Illusions

Sunsets painted in soft pastels,
Whispering winds through autumn leaves,
Gentle hues where magic dwells,
Artistry that time deceives.

Rainbows melt in morning dew,
Lilac skies with tints of rose,
Mirrored lakes reflect the view,
Dreamscapes only hearts disclose.

Butterflies in twilight's dance,
Wings aglow in tender light,
Moments held in sweet romance,
Lasting through the quiet night.

Seas of lavender and blush,
Cascades fall with silken grace,
Nature's canvas painted lush,
Every stroke a warm embrace.

Whispered dreams in colors fade,
Pastel realms of calm allure,
In this space where magic's made,
Worlds of wonder still endure.

Visions in Vibrant Hues

Crimson dawns and amber skies,
Verdant fields and sapphire seas,
Journey where pure color lies,
In this realm, all spirits ease.

Bold strokes paint the world anew,
Mountains robed in emerald sheen,
Vivid dreams in every hue,
Liveliness in each new scene.

Sunflowers reach for the sun,
Petals bathed in golden glow,
Nature's call where life's begun,
Colors set our hearts aglow.

Evening paints in twilight's brush,
Shades of purple, red, and blue,
Silent moments, time's soft hush,
Visions clear and ever true.

Rainfalls dance on lush terrains,
Harmonies of red and green,
Life in vibrant hues sustains,
In this splendidly serene.

Awake in a Watercolor

Morning breaks in soft pastel,
Brushstrokes on a canvas wide,
Whispers of a dream to tell,
Awakening the artist's pride.

Mountains loom in gentle gray,
Rivers weave in shades of blue,
Every dawn a new display,
Every hue a story new.

Clouds drift in a lilac sea,
Skies pour out their golden light,
In this realm of mystery,
Day and night in seamless flight.

Trees take on a varied hue,
Shadows play in green and gold,
Nature in her form so true,
Stories in her heart unfold.

Each moment crafted by the hand,
Of a painter wise and free,
In this watercolor land,
Colors breathe in harmony.

Lush Skies of Imagination

In the realm where dreams alight,
Colors blend in sheer delight.
Whispers of the stars ignite,
A journey through the endless night.

Winds of wonder softly play,
Guiding hearts to distant day.
In the azure's vast array,
Hopes are born and gently sway.

Visions weave in cosmic streams,
Painting lands of boundless dreams.
Every spark a thought redeems,
In the skies where freedom teems.

Beyond the clouds, a boundless sea,
Ideas dance, forever free.
In that realm where thoughts can be,
Lush skies cradle fantasy.

Surreal Serenity

Whispers of a tranquil breeze,
Through the fields and past the trees.
Worlds of calm and silent seas,
In serenity's gentle ease.

Glowing dusk, a golden hue,
Nature paints in subtle cues.
Dreams of peace in colors true,
With each touch, a life anew.

Harmony in night's embrace,
Stars in silent, sacred space.
Echoes of a softer pace,
Time's sweet flow, a tender grace.

In the heart of quiet streams,
Life resides in peaceful themes.
Surreal realms of tranquil dreams,
Where the purest silence gleams.

Canvas Odyssey

Brushes glide on canvas bare,
Stories woven in the air.
Hues of life in colors rare,
Tales untold of dreams we share.

Strokes of passion, shades of night,
Moments captured in the light.
Every color, every fight,
In this canvas, pure, bright.

Journeys of the heart and soul,
Through the brush, the painter's goal.
In each line, a hidden scroll,
Every piece, a whispered whole.

Within the frame, the worlds collide,
Depths of time and space reside.
On this voyage, hearts confide,
In the art, we'll long abide.

Moonlit Masterpieces

Underneath the silver moon,
Dreams are crafted, quiet, soon.
In the still of midnight's tune,
Art is born, a distant boon.

Stars align to inspire grace,
In their light, the artist's place.
Beauty found in every trace,
Painted with a gentle pace.

Moonlight glows on silent trees,
Whispers' brush on subtle breeze.
In the night, the heart appease,
Masterpieces, moments seize.

Shadows dance in twilight's gleam,
Echoes of a timeless theme.
In the night where visions teem,
Art and moon, a perfect dream.

Nocturnal Narratives

Beneath a moon kissed velvet sky,
Whispers of dreams drift gently by.
Owls serenade the night's embrace,
Stars recount tales of endless space.

Midnight winds weave through silent trees,
Echoing ancient mysteries.
Crickets compose a twilight tune,
Waltzing shadows in the pale moon.

From dusk till dawn, the stories spin,
As fireflies' glow illuminates within.
In nocturnal hues, the magic weaves,
A tapestry of myths conceived.

When slumber calls with a silken thread,
Rest your eyes, lay down your head.
For in the night, the world seems vast,
Nocturnal dreams forever cast.

Abstract Dreams

In realms where colors lose their bounds,
Silence speaks with mystic sounds.
Shapes dissolve in fluid streams,
Floating through abstract dreams.

Time unravels in loops of gold,
Stories within stories folded.
Whispers brush the outstretched beams,
Painting thoughts in abstract dreams.

Paths of light and shadow blend,
Journeys with no start or end.
Imagination's quivering seams,
Stitched in threads of abstract dreams.

Unfathomed depths of tireless skies,
Where questions dwell and seldom lies.
Reality bends and softly gleams,
In the heart of abstract dreams.

Strokes of Whimsy

Brushes dipped in rainbow hues,
Dance across the canvas blues.
Imaginations swirl and sway,
In a whimsical cabaret.

From each stroke a story flows,
Tales of laughter, joy, and woes.
Castles float on cotton clouds,
Penguins sing, and flowers crowds.

Each line weaves a fantasy,
Captured in a symphony.
Unicorns with pastel wings,
Whisper secrets through the springs.

In this realm of whimsy bright,
Every color shares its light.
Dreams are painted with pure glee,
In strokes of endless whimsy.

Fantasy on Canvas

Dragons soar through twilight skies,
Magic sparkles in their eyes.
Forests whisper ancient rhymes,
Passed down through enchanted times.

Princesses in towers old,
Stories of their courage told.
Knights in armor, brave and true,
Guard the realms of skies so blue.

Seas of wonder, tales untold,
Mermaids swim in deepest gold.
Mystic lands of dreams enhance,
For each brushstroke is a dance.

Every color tells a tale,
Fairy wings and ships set sail.
On this canvas, worlds arise,
Fantasy within our eyes.

Chasing Phantoms in Paint

Brushes sweep in silent dance,
Colors blend in muted trance.
Shadows creep, a fluid gait,
Chasing phantoms, tempting fate.

Shapes emerge from darkest hue,
Whispers tell of what they knew.
Every stroke, a ghostly flight,
Drawing visions in the night.

Veil of mist on canvas drawn,
Echoes linger, dusk to dawn.
Elusive forms in secret plight,
Cloaked in mystery, out of sight.

Fleeting glimpses, shadows play,
In the twilight's soft array.
Captured spirits, tales untold,
Chasing phantoms, slick and bold.

Silhouettes in haunting grace,
Woven in this quiet space.
Art transcends beyond the norm,
In pursuit, the phantoms swarm.

Midnight Masterpieces

Beneath the moon's soft, silver gleam,
Artists dream in endless stream.
Midnight calls and whispers low,
Guiding hands in mystic flow.

Stars ignite creative furls,
Celestial paths in cosmic swirls.
Brushes dance and hues converse,
Crafting realms beyond the curse.

Silent echoes fill the night,
Guiding strokes with gentle light.
Breathing life in darkened hues,
Midnight brings the muse its dues.

Canvas washed in twilight's shade,
Every line a starlit braid.
In the stillness, visions rise,
Colors mirrored in the skies.

Masterpieces softly born,
In the cradle of the morn.
Midnight's touch, a tender gift,
Bringing dreams on shadows' lift.

Dreamy Dimensions

Beneath the surface, worlds unfold,
In vibrant tales of bold and old.
Dreams distilled in liquid light,
Weaving through the velvet night.

Realms within a single breath,
Colors born from shades of depth.
Fantasy in fractal lines,
Dimensions wrapped in cryptic signs.

Harmonies in silent streams,
Where the mind's eye softly gleams.
Parallel in whispered grace,
Sensations bloom in boundless space.

Illusions form and gently break,
In the canvas, new worlds wake.
Every dream a deeper call,
Dimensions drift, embracing all.

Fluid realms of thought and sight,
Wings unfurled in endless flight.
In these dreamy, boundless seas,
New dimensions set us free.

Spectral Canvases

Ghostly fingers trace the air,
In a dance both rare and fair.
Canvas whispers silent tales,
Of spectral hues and mystic veils.

Pale as morning's softest breath,
Hues of life, defying death.
Spirit strokes in twilight's shade,
Ephemeral, they gently fade.

Glimmers of forgotten light,
Softly paint the edges bright.
Shadowed forms in subtle grace,
Haunting every hidden space.

Timeless echoes softly play,
In the painter's quiet sway.
Veiled figures in repose,
On the spectral canvas pose.

Mystic scenes in gentle flow,
Captured in the twilight's glow.
Ghostly visions softly blend,
In a dance that has no end.

Nights in Oil and Acrylic

Stars bleed colors in twilight's frame,
Brush strokes whisper a poet's name,
Canvas of dreams where shadows play,
Midnight hues chase the light away.

Luminous drips on an inky sheet,
Palette knives dance in rhythms sweet,
Vivid tales of nocturnal flight,
Captured in hues of endless night.

Ponderous skies in swirls of thought,
Each pigment, passions dearly bought,
Constellations in painted scheme,
Woven into an artist's dream.

Dark ensnares with a gentle grace,
Lines converge in a silent space,
Muses linger in spectral light,
Breathing life into the depth of night.

Daydream Diptych

Sunlight spills in golden streams,
Awaking worlds of whispered dreams,
Thoughts cascade in vibrant hue,
Daydreams crafted in skies so blue.

Lavender clouds on a canvas broad,
Horizons painted by nature's god,
Timeless tales in the light of day,
Whisking wanderers far away.

Periwinkle fields of daisy white,
In morning's grace, hearts take flight,
Ethereal paths in the dazzle of dawn,
Traced by the hand of a restless fawn.

In every streak, a wish released,
Fleeting yet never fully ceased,
Bathe in the glow of bright midday,
Lost in reverie, gone astray.

Spectral Symphony

Echoes of colors in spectral bands,
Whisper symphonies with unseen hands,
Rays of light through prisms' fight,
Painting a tune in visible flight.

Harmony in the hue's embrace,
Chords in the light, a soft carapace,
Resonant tones in silent leagues,
Soundless yet vibrant in its intrigue.

Aurora sways in a chromatic waltz,
Delightful errors with no faults,
Every note in the rainbow's gleam,
Part of a boundless, living theme.

Dissolving dusk in twilight's tear,
Auroras play as stars appear,
Silhouetted spectres softly sing,
In the dark's gentle, encompassing wing.

Impressionistic Nightfall

Twilight blurs with a stolen kiss,
Hues of jade in a world of bliss,
Brushes carve the evening's tale,
Moonlight dances, shadows pale.

Stars emerge in a soft ballet,
Color melts in a twilight play,
Horizon's edge in blurred delight,
Melancholy whispers in the night.

Impressions deep with each stroke true,
Dreamscapes born in an indigo hue,
Chiaroscuro of often forgot,
Memoirs of night in an artist's thought.

Veils of nightfall, soft and deep,
Cradle the world in a gentle sleep,
Canvas dreams in a blue embrace,
In nocturne's hand, find their place.

Painter's Midnight Reveries

Under the moon's soft, silver glow,
The artist dreams with canvas wide,
Brush in hand, to realms they'll go,
Colors blend where stars reside.

Midnight whispers to the soul,
Each stroke a dance in silent night,
Hues of dreams begin to roll,
Creating worlds in soft twilight.

In the quiet, shadows play,
Musing forms that drift and weave,
Endless skies of blue and gray,
Patterns only night conceive.

From the dark, a light will spring,
Glimmers of an artist's mind,
Wonders pure, forever sing,
Captured moments unconfined.

When the dawn begins to break,
A masterpiece in morning's light,
Shows the journey artists take,
Painting dreams in deepest night.

Sketches of Slumber

Close your eyes to nighttime's grace,
Lulled to rest by shadows deep,
Softly now, in dreams' embrace,
Sketches form as you drift to sleep.

Whispers from the twilight shore,
Bring to mind a silent tune,
Drawn in lines forevermore,
In the stillness of the moon.

Gentle arcs and subtle hues,
Waves of thought in quiet sway,
Fill the night with tranquil views,
Sleeping hours slide away.

Contours blend and shapes emerge,
Visions seen through closed eyelids,
Sketches, as the dreams converge,
Weave a tapestry of skids.

When the dawn begins to rise,
And the morning light is true,
Dreamland sketches realize,
Bringing slumber's art to view.

Chasing Painted Fantasies

Running through a canvas wide,
Chasing hues that drift and spin,
Rivers of a world inside,
Where every brushstroke's breath begins.

Bright illusions take their flight,
Sweeping reds and gold collide,
Dreams unfold with wild delight,
In a landscape not denied.

Each new color whispers quick,
Secrets of a fleeting dream,
Every shade a heartbeat's flick,
Every tone a silken seam.

Hopes and fears are intertwined,
Captured in the painted chase,
Ethereal and so refined,
Fantasy in soft embrace.

Till the final touch is made,
And the colors find their peace,
The painted dreams begin to fade,
Leaving echoes that won't cease.

Whispers in Color

Silent strokes on canvas bare,
Whispers softly paint the night,
Hushed confessions fill the air,
Crafting scenes of pure delight.

Palette whispers secrets round,
Blending shades in soft caress,
Lost in tones where dreams are found,
Colors weave a gentle press.

Brightest yellows, deepest blues,
Speak of sunlight and of sea,
Vivid reds in whispered hues,
Tell of passion wild and free.

Each new layer's muted sound,
Sings a song of silent grace,
Whispers in the colors bound,
Trace the lines of time and space.

When the whispers come to end,
And the work is finished, whole,
Silent stories they will send,
Lingering in every soul.

Imaginative Realms

In lands where thoughts take shape,
Mountains built from whispers faint,
Rivers of dreams gently drape,
Through valleys of colored paint.

Skies painted with notions bright,
Oceans deep with musings blend,
Stars narrate through soft moonlight,
Tales that no words can amend.

Forests of unspoken deeds,
Swirl in winds of untold lore,
Paths that mark dreamers' creeds,
Lead to gates of unknown door.

Birds sing songs of phantom bloom,
Clouds cradle flights of wild care,
Fields where endless fancies loom,
Wanderers rest in twilight's fare.

Bridges built by fantasy's hand,
Towers of belief brightly gleam,
In this boundless, surreal land,
We dwell within figments of a dream.

Dreamscapes Unveiled

Through the veil of silent sleep,
Worlds awaken, softly spun,
Visions there in shadows creep,
Unfurling beneath the moon and sun.

Whispers of the stars' delight,
Patterns weave in twilight's air,
Glimpses of the dreams take flight,
In vistas strange yet fair.

Oft we wander paths unknown,
Hand in hand with phantoms kind,
In realms where the seeds are sown,
Of stories woven in the mind.

Waves of thought beneath night's dome,
Wash ashore with hushed appeal,
In a land that calls us home,
Where only our hearts kneel.

Echoes of the unvoiced past,
Resonate in silent night,
In dreams where our spirits cast,
Our hidden hopes in spectral light.

Chromatic Reveries

Colors blend in twilight's kiss,
Pastel whispers fill the air,
In the dawn's soft, radiant bliss,
A canvas painted with care.

Rainbows arch in sky's embrace,
Hues of dreams splashed far and wide,
Brushstrokes of a silent grace,
In the heart of night they bide.

In the gardens of our sleep,
Blossoms bloom in endless shade,
Each tulip sings a secret deep,
In tones of twilight's parade.

Palettes lit by moon's soft beam,
Mingle with the sun's old hues,
In this world where colors dream,
We walk as they diffuse.

Tints and shades of our design,
Merge in prisms of our sighs,
In the twilight's gleam divine,
Truths of mind materialize.

Sleepwalking with Paint

Silent footsteps in the night,
Brushes whisper on the wood,
Dreams in color take their flight,
In twilight's magical hood.

Shadows dance with forms undrawn,
Pigments pulse in mystic flow,
Figures born at breaking dawn,
To surreal realms we'll go.

Palettes speak in vivid tales,
On the canvas of our dreams,
Each new stroke our thoughts unveil,
Crafting realms of moonlit gleams.

Textures weave a twilight song,
Upon the silent veil of thought,
Walking where the dreams belong,
In the artful worlds we've sought.

In the stillness paint does breathe,
Whispering secrets deep and quaint,
As we wander, minds unsheathe,
While sleepwalking with paint.

Chromatic Chimeras

In twilight's grasp, the colors blur,
Where dreams and reality confer,
A fusion dance of light's attire,
In hues that set the soul afire.

Spectral creatures weave and whirl,
In cosmic depths where shadows curl,
Their forms a tapestry of grace,
Alive in night's embrace.

Through prisms, visions intertwine,
A kaleidoscope of the divine,
Chimeras wrought from color streams,
Awakened from our lucid dreams.

In every shade a story told,
Of beauty fierce, and whispers bold,
Chromatic realms where echoes play,
And night submits to day.

Let pigments breathe in silent roar,
As twilight chimes forevermore,
To paint the sky in sublime arcs,
Where chimeras leave their marks.

Between Sleep and Spectra

In the twilight's gentle hue,
Where moonlight lingers, soft and true,
A realm between the sleep and wake,
Where dreams like specters softly break.

Stars whisper secrets to the night,
Guiding souls in spectral flight,
Through veils of mist, the visions flow,
In colors only night can know.

Shadows weave in moonlit streams,
Crafting realms from silent dreams,
Between the realms where silence reigns,
And consciousness unchains.

Each breath a bridge to worlds unseen,
Where waking thoughts and dreams convene,
In this serene and spectral space,
Time itself must slow its pace.

So wander free, where night is deep,
Between the spectra and the sleep,
Let every shadow, spectral gleam,
Illuminate your deepest dream.

Imaginary Brushwork

With each stroke, the canvas sighs,
Where colors dance, and spirit flies,
An artist's dream in vivid hue,
Imagined worlds come into view.

Brushes whisper secrets old,
Crafting stories in the bold,
Lines that curve and shades that blend,
A universe at the painter's end.

Imagination runs astray,
In swirling mist, the pigments play,
Visions birthed from creative core,
Alive forevermore.

In every hue, a tale resides,
Where fantasy and truth collide,
A brush's sweep, a breath of grace,
Defining form in empty space.

Let strokes of dream caress the night,
And bring the shadows into light,
For in each artful flick, we see,
Imaginary brushwork, wild and free.

Whimsy in Washes

In watercolor's gentle flow,
Whimsy's born in softest glow,
A dance of hues in liquid blend,
Where reality and fancy bend.

Clouds of cerulean drift with ease,
In meadows brushed with autumn's breeze,
Whispering tales to quiet streams,
That wander through our dreams.

Every drop, a gentle kiss,
Transforming blank to vibrant bliss,
With washes of the light and dark,
Creation leaves its mark.

Through the splendor, joy is found,
In puddles where the colors mound,
A playful touch in every hue,
Where whimsy comes to view.

So let your heart by colors be,
And paint the world in fantasy,
For in the washes gently spread,
Lives whimsy's tender thread.

Ethereal Easel

Upon the canvas, dreams do hum,
Brushstrokes weave, a world begun.
Colors merge, a nebula bright,
In shadows deep and stars of night.

Hues of fire, gentle streams,
Mirroring our endless dreams.
Silent whispers, soft as dawn,
In twilight's glow, the veil withdrawn.

Mountains rise in mists of gold,
Winds of time their tales unfold.
Oceans speak in gentle sighs,
Dancing under starlit skies.

Ethereal shapes drift and sway,
In the artist's touch, they play.
Every stroke a ghostly scene,
Bound within this painted dream.

Infinite voids, light and shade,
On the easel, the universe laid.
Creation sings in silent grace,
In the masterpiece, we find our place.

Ink-Dreamed Vistas

Ink murmurs on the blank expanse,
Weaving tales in shadowed dance.
Visions bloom in twilight's gleam,
Crafted from the inkwell's dream.

Whispers of forgotten lore,
Emerge from depths, forevermore.
Mountains carved in midnight's hue,
Under skies of inky blue.

Rivers carved by quill and pen,
Flow through valleys now and then.
Each line drawn with tender grace,
Sketches from a world in space.

Forests rise in sable night,
Bathed in soft, unearthly light.
Creatures roam in mystic flight,
In this realm of ink-born sight.

Yet as the dawn begins to break,
Ink and dreams their leave shall take.
Fading vistas, solace yearn,
'Til the ink dreams shall return.

The Phantom Painter

Silent hands in moonlit beams,
Craft ethereal, silent dreams.
Shadows dance upon the frame,
Whispering the phantom's name.

Figures born of mist and light,
In the quiet of the night.
On canvas, they softly gleam,
Woven from the artist's dream.

Reaching through the darkened veil,
Spirits tell their setless tale.
Each stroke speaks of memories old,
In ghostly hues of silver and gold.

The phantom's touch, so light, so thin,
Breathes life to worlds that lie within.
Every shade a mystery,
Painted in lost history.

When at last, the night does fade,
The phantom's art begins to shade.
Yet in the echoes of the past,
Their painted works forever last.

Canvas Nocturne

In the calm of midnight's reign,
Form and color break the chain.
Softly, then, the brush does trace,
Moonlit scenes in velvet space.

Stars are pinned in endless night,
Silver glows in quiet light.
Mountains kissed by shadows deep,
Under canvas skies, they sleep.

Waves that shimmer, softly crest,
In painted dreams, they find their rest.
Birdsong whispers, barely heard,
In this night, the soul is stirred.

Echoes of a twilight dream,
Gently flow in final theme.
Every hue a somber hymn,
Drawing on the night's dark rim.

As dawn begins to weave its thread,
Nighttime hues in silence shed.
Yet through the day, still shall remain,
The nocturne's soul in quiet refrain.

Mystic Mediums

In twilight's gentle, secret shroud,
Where whispers of the night are proud,
The mystics dance with hidden grace,
In realms where time suspends its pace.

Through veils of mist, they weave their dreams,
In moonlit pools and silver streams,
With ancient lore and subtle art,
They mend the threads of broken heart.

An echo of an ancient song,
In seers' eyes that gaze so long,
Their wisdom flows through realms unseen,
A tapestry of worlds between.

The stars align with messages,
Encoded rhyme in verbal sieges,
In silent chants, their power grows,
And through their craft, the future shows.

From dusk till dawn, their magic spins,
A timeless dance where fate begins,
Mystic mediums, their secrets blend,
In twilight's hush, where visions mend.

Journeys in Hue

In dawn's embrace, the colors wake,
With hues that light and shadows shake,
A palette birthed in morning's breath,
A symphony of life's fair wraith.

From scarlet dawn to azure day,
Through golden fields and skies of gray,
The journey finds its vibrant tune,
In bloom of rose and gentle lune.

Emerald forests, oceans blue,
With every step, a different view,
In every hue, a story blends,
Of cosmic paths and mortal ends.

The twilight brings a spectrum bright,
As stars burst forth in velvet night,
With every shade, the world is spun,
A prism's path till day is done.

In dreams we travel, colors sway,
Through prisms that the night displays,
Journeys in hue, a boundless sea,
Of endless beauty, wild and free.

Fantasque Figures

In twilight's theatre, shadows play,
With forms that twist in light's array,
The stage is set in dreams surreal,
Where figures move with painted zeal.

Fantastical, their dances weave,
Through realms our waking minds conceive,
With steps that trill in foreign lands,
And gestures wrought by unseen hands.

Their eyes, a spark of distant stars,
Reflecting moons and Venus' scars,
In costumes bright or spectral bare,
They carve out stories in the air.

Unknown their scripts, yet clear their tale,
Of wanderlust and heartfelt trail,
In whispered songs and silent calls,
Their mystic art, the soul enthralls.

In every twirl, a secret spins,
Of hidden worlds and hidden sins,
Fantasque figures take their flight,
In twilight's dream, through endless night.

Visionary Veils

Beneath the veil of starlit sight,
The visions bloom in quiet night,
They whisper truths and secrets keep,
In realms where waking minds can't leap.

Soft veils of dreams and misty glow,
Through which the future's facets show,
A woven web of hopes and fears,
In silent dance through fleeting years.

Infinity in veils revealed,
With stories of the heart unsealed,
Through translucent dreams, they guide the way,
Across the night to break of day.

Each veil a layer deep and wise,
Reflecting echoes of the skies,
Their wisdom speaks without a sound,
In visions pure and profound.

In shadows cast by moon's soft gleams,
The visionary dance in seams,
Of twilight's cloak, where secrets pave,
A path through night's enchanted wave.

Canvas of Nightfall

As twilight drapes the sky in hues of blue,
The stars emerge, a silken-threaded view.
Whispers of moonlight paint the silent seas,
Where shadows dance with grace among the trees.

The world in softest shades begins to glow,
A symphony of peace in evening's flow.
Each breath of night, a brushstroke in the air,
A tranquil scene, a moment pure and rare.

Beneath the velvet canopy's embrace,
The dreams of dusk find harmony and grace.
Time slows its march, and hearts begin to sigh,
Embraced by night's soft lullaby.

As constellations weave their ancient tales,
The earth beneath them quiet, calm, prevails.
A galaxy in whispers gently calls,
And bids us dream through night's celestial halls.

Dappled Dreams

In realms where sunlight filters through the leaves,
A tapestry of light and shadow weaves.
Each ray a golden thread in nature's seams,
Awakening the land in dappled dreams.

The whisper of the winds through branches high,
A lullaby beneath the azure sky.
The rustle of the leaves, a soft retreat,
A peaceful rhythm where the earth and air meet.

Meadows sway in harmonies unseen,
A chorus of the wild, serene and clean.
Each petal, blade, and bough in unity,
A vision of unspoken poetry.

As daylight fades to twilight's gentle gleam,
The world transforms in hues of deeper dream.
In dappled light and shadow, we are free,
To wander through night's calm tranquillity.

Spectral Sketches

In twilight's tender glow, the shadows play,
A dance of phantoms on their worldly way.
With whispers soft, they sketch the evening's tale,
In hues of silver, soft and frail.

The moon, an artist in the velvet sky,
With beams of light, creates where dark things lie.
Each glow a stroke, a spectral, silent trace,
That paints the world in night's embrace.

Beneath its touch, the world becomes serene,
A canvas dark yet touched with gentle sheen.
Through spectral sketches, dreams begin to form,
In twilight's still, unending calm.

The stars, like watchful eyes, observe the scene,
In night's embrace, both misty and serene.
Each moment etched in quiet, silver hues,
A masterpiece the night alone can choose.

Nocturnal Creations

When day surrenders to the cloak of night,
The world transforms beneath the moon's soft light.
In shadowed corners, dreams begin to rise,
Nocturnal creations, seen through sleepless eyes.

The silence speaks in whispers to the soul,
A voice from stars that makes the spirit whole.
Each twinkle, like a word, in dark's embrace,
Conveys a tale of endless space.

The night unfolds its mysteries unseen,
In shades of black, blue, and silver sheen.
Each breath of wind, a note in night's own song,
A melody that carries us along.

With every moment, night invents anew,
A world of dreams where moments are but few.
In nocturnal creations, hearts find peace,
And sweet embrace as night's wonders increase.

Spectral Stories

In moonlit whispers, shadows lace,
With secrets spun by stars' embrace.
Veils of night, a ghostly guise,
Where history's echoes softly rise.

Lost in twilight's gentle sweep,
Dreams awaken from their sleep.
Phantoms dance in twilight's grace,
In haunted realms, they find their place.

Through ancient woods where echoes play,
Ghostly tales lead hearts astray.
Silhouettes of long-lost time,
Emerge in twilight's mystic rhyme.

Spectral voices, soft and chaste,
In this realm, their presence traced.
Timeless whispers fill the air,
Tales of wonder, dark and rare.

In the quiet, shadows sing,
Of forgotten loves that time did bring.
Beneath the stars, where stories rest,
Lay spectral dreams at twilight's crest.

Luminous Lull

Beneath the sky of velvet hue,
Stars awaken, fill the view.
Soft as dreams, their light does weave,
A lullaby for hearts to cleave.

Moonbeams dance on tranquil seas,
Casting shadows, whispering breeze.
In the hush of night's embrace,
Luminous dreams find their space.

Slumber's web in silver spun,
Threads the night till day is done.
Crystal visions float on high,
In the canvas of the sky.

Softly sings the cosmic tune,
Lulled by stars and gentle moon.
Hearts on wander, souls take flight,
Guided by the tranquil light.

In this realm where night holds sway,
Dreams unfold in wondrous play.
Luminous paths through worlds unknown,
In sleep's embrace, we are shown.

Enchanted Easel

Painted dreams on canvas bright,
Brush of magic, hues of light.
Whispers of enchanted lands,
Brought to life by artist's hands.

Twilight's colors softly blend,
Crafting scenes where dreams ascend.
Mystic realms within a frame,
Where illusion has a name.

Textures speak of tales unheard,
Silent songs in every word.
Strokes of mystery, bound by grace,
An enchanted world in endless chase.

With each stroke, a story grows,
Life in colors gently flows.
Easel calls with siren's cry,
To realms where fantasy flies high.

Through this portal, visions fly,
Beneath a never-changing sky.
Imagination takes its stand,
In the artist's gentle hand.

Dali-esque Dwellings

Surreal skies in fractured dawn,
Worlds of wonder fading, gone.
Twisting forms that float on breeze,
In Dali's dream, time's echoes freeze.

Melting clocks and limpid skies,
Abstract truths in subtle guise.
Warped and tangled, dreams unfold,
A liquid scene, both brave and bold.

In the canvas, landscapes bend,
Shifting shapes that never end.
Rhythms of a mind untamed,
In this space, all truths are claimed.

Palaces of melting gold,
Whispers of the unreal told.
Strange and wondrous, life refrains,
In these realms where Dali reigns.

Each dimension, soft and free,
Holds a piece of mystery.
In this dreamscape, minds entwine,
In Dali's world of the divine.

Essence of Nightshade

Beneath the moon's eternal gaze,
Where shadows twist and turn in haze,
Nightshade blooms in silent grace,
A hidden realm in dark embrace.

Whispers float on midnight breeze,
Mystic scents that minds appease,
Stars like eyes in velvet seas,
Guard the night with patient ease.

In the void, where dreams reside,
Petals spill like secrets wide,
Unfolding tales with every stride,
Nightshade's beauty never hides.

Contours blur in dusky shroud,
Silence wraps like twilight's crowd,
Nature's whispers, soft yet loud,
Midnight's garden, dark and proud.

Ephemeral and so profound,
In the night, where truths abound,
Nightshade weaves through time unbound,
Silent echoes, a profound sound.

Mythic Mosaics

In lands where legends find their birth,
Tales are woven, rich in worth,
Mythic wings spread through the earth,
Fragments lost, tales of mirth.

Warriors brave and fates entwined,
Gods and mortals, realms aligned,
Mosaics of a timeless kind,
Mystic truths that hearts remind.

Dragons breathe with ancient fire,
Spires that touch the stars aspire,
Magic stirs and dreams conspire,
Binding hearts with rare desire.

Oceans deep with secrets keep,
Siren songs through currents sweep,
In mythic dreams we fall, then leap,
Awakened by the stories' deep.

Mosaics danced by silver light,
Etched in souls through darkest night,
In every tale, a flash of bright,
Mythic whispers taking flight.

Unseen Landscapes

Beyond the veil of sighted bounds,
Where silence sings and space surrounds,
Unseen landscapes softly sound,
Worlds within the mind are found.

Textures born of thought and haze,
Colours shift in endless maze,
Dreams and visions intertwine,
Crafting realms where imag'ry plays.

Mountains rise from whispered streams,
Forests birthed in twilight beams,
Valleys curve in fluid seams,
Unseen realms of endless dreams.

Oceans stirred by unseen storms,
Deserts where the spirit warms,
Unseen landscapes, boundless forms,
Wandered in the mind's reformed.

Journeys where the heart's at home,
Travelling through spaceless dome,
In unseen landscapes, free to roam,
A universe within our own.

Brushstrokes of Reverie

Canvas wide and colours bright,
Dreams unfold in morning light,
Brushstrokes weave a tale in flight,
Reveries dance in pure delight.

Every hue a whispered dream,
Every line a silver beam,
Brushstrokes soft as silken stream,
Shapes and shadows, light and gleam.

In the strokes, the soul reveals,
Wounds and joys, it gently heals,
Brushstrokes paint what heart conceals,
Depths of feeling, mind's ideals.

Horizons blend with sky and sea,
Trees that sing in harmony,
Brushstrokes capture fantasy,
Art and life in unity.

A world is born in every swipe,
Lands of legend, scenes so ripe,
Brushstrokes tell our dreams, our type,
In reverie, we find the hype.

Impressions of the Mind

In silent rooms, thoughts intertwine,
A dance of echoes, vast, divine,
Ideas flutter, bold and shy,
Beneath the canvas of the sky.

Wisps of dreams in shadows cast,
Memories linger, holding fast,
Through veils of time, they roam afar,
Each one a tale, each one a scar.

Silent symphony, whispers' song,
A harmony forgotten long,
In every corner, nooks confined,
Lies treasures of the restless mind.

Infinite worlds within us glow,
Rivers of thought begin to flow,
Through night and day, in dark or light,
They sculpt our soul with sheer delight.

In mazes deep, we leave a mark,
Guided by an inner spark,
An odyssey to realms unknown,
The mind's creation, all our own.

Captured Whispers

In twilight's embrace, secrets stay,
Whispers echoed, night and day,
Through silent winds, they softly go,
In moonlit beams, they faintly glow.

Veiled in shadows, words of grace,
Hints of stories that time can't erase,
From lips to ears, the gentle glide,
In whispered tones, the truths reside.

Beneath the stars, in hushed delight,
Dreams take flight in the still of night,
A symphony of thoughts, unseen,
In every pause, a space between.

Voices linger on the breeze,
Their messages carried with such ease,
From soul to soul, a bridge they make,
In whispered vows, we all partake.

Unseen rivers flow through air,
With secrets only few could bear,
Captured whispers, evermore,
An endless dance on time's own shore.

Fanciful Pigments

Brush in hand, with strokes of flair,
Colors burst through morning air,
A canvas dressed in dreams outspread,
Life in every vibrant thread.

Cobalt skies and emerald streams,
Blend with sunlight's golden beams,
Petals whisper hues untold,
Boundless stories, rich and bold.

Dancing shades in twilight's glow,
Paint the secrets we all know,
Every hue a silent song,
Echoes of where hearts belong.

Palette teems with endless sights,
A symphony in pure delights,
Each new stroke a boundless tale,
In fanciful pigments, we set sail.

Through days and nights, creations gleam,
Crafted from a wandering dream,
In every tone, in every shade,
Our spirits flow, forever laid.

Hues of the Heart

In love's embrace, the colors gleam,
With every shade, a woven dream,
Crimson pulses, passion's beat,
In tender moments, bittersweet.

Azure whispers, calm and wide,
Echoes of a deep inside,
Through tides of time, emotions part,
Unveiling shades within the heart.

Golden glimmers, joy's delight,
Fleeting as the morning light,
In every hue, a story spun,
By threads of hearts, forever spun.

In violet dusk and amber morn,
Feelings rise, anew, reborn,
A spectrum vast, where love takes flight,
Through shades of heart, to endless height.

In every color, love's own thread,
Weaves through nights and dawns ahead,
Hues of the heart, in light, in dark,
A timeless canvas, our souls mark.

Ink of the Subconscious

When night unfurls its dusky sails,
The mind begins a silent quest.
In realms where daylight's logic fails,
The ink of dreams writes vivid zest.

Unseen forces guide dark quills,
Sketching tales of untamed lands.
Within these sheets our desires spill,
A world drawn by hidden hands.

Symbols float in fluid streams,
Tales half-seen yet deeply felt.
Through fluid lines of fractured dreams,
Subconscious depths begin to melt.

Visions born from shadow's mind,
Traced by whispers, soft yet clear.
In this ink, new paths we'll find,
A canvas broad, where thoughts revere.

As dawn approaches, worlds regress,
Into the void of waking light.
Yet still the ink remains to bless,
A tether to our dream-filled night.

Abstract Nightscapes

Stars are whispers in the dark,
Silent notes of cosmic art.
Each luminous flick, a brighten'd spark,
Abstract strokes from night's vast heart.

Planets waltz through endless skies,
Choreographed in shadow's dome.
Their paths a dance of hidden ties,
Nightscapes where our dreams may roam.

Nebulas like splattered inks,
Crafted by celestial hand.
A canvas where perception sinks,
Into the depths of dream's command.

Galaxies in spiral forms,
Stretching far beyond our sight.
Within their swirls, untold norms,
Abstract tales of endless night.

As we gaze in silent awe,
Lost within this cosmic sprawl.
Our minds unshackle from the law,
Of daylight's grip, night claims us all.

Visionary Hues

In the artist's vibrant mind,
Colors pulse in rhythmic beat.
With each stroke, new worlds we find,
Visionary hues, pure and sweet.

Palette's dance of endless dreams,
Brush of thought on canvas laid.
Every hue like liquid beams,
A vivid world in spectrum made.

In shadows, secrets softly hide,
Contours shaped by light's embrace.
Through hues, raw emotions ride,
Art that time cannot erase.

Blues of calm and reds of fire,
Blend to form a visual song.
Visionary hues inspire,
A realm where all dreams belong.

As the masterpiece unfolds,
We stand entranced by colors' play.
Through these hues, the heart beholds,
A visionary bright display.

Cradled in Creation

In the arms of endless thought,
Creation cradles like a child.
With each idea, new worlds are brought,
Where imagination runs wild.

From the void, forms begin to rise,
Crafted by inventive minds.
Inspiration never lies,
In its grasp, pure magic finds.

Birthing stars from simple sparks,
Dreams take shape, a brave new form.
In creation's gentle arcs,
Fantasies in hearts are warm.

Hands that mold with loving care,
Craft existence, pure and bright.
In the cradle, infinite and rare,
Creation breathes in morning light.

As these worlds from thought emerge,
Boundless, free from earthly ties.
In creation's tender surge,
Our spirits lift, our souls arise.

Milton Keynes UK
Ingram Content Group UK Ltd.
UKHW021029230724
445880UK00003B/24